ROCKIN' CHRISTMAS

FOR 5-STRING BASS

**THE MOST POPULAR
CHRISTMAS SONGS ARRANGED
FOR 5-STRING BASS
INCLUDING DUETS, BASS
CHORD DIAGRAMS, AND
TWO-HAND TAPPING**

B Y   B R I A N   E M M E L

Cover Art - Eddie Young
Typesetting - Derek Cornett
Paste-up - Cindy Middlebrook

ISBN 0-931759-89-7
SAN 683-8022

Copyright © 1994 CENTERSTREAM Publishing
P.O. Box 5450 - Fullerton CA 52935
All rights for publication and distribution are reserved. No part of this book may be reproduced in any form or by any
electronic or mechanical means including information storage and retrieval systems without permission in
writing from the publisher, except by reviewers who may quote brief passages in review.

Contents

The Author

Brian Emmel was born and raised in northern Ohio. He moved to Los Angeles in the summer of 1988, where he began his official music career. He graduated from Musician's Institute (B.I.T.) in Hollywood, graduating in the top class. He has written three other books for Centerstream Publishing, **"5 string Bass Method", "Scales and Modes for the 5 string Bass"** and **"Creating Rhythm Styles for 5 string Bass with Drum accompaniment"**.

Brian formed the rock band "SirReal" in the latter months of 1991 and played local L.A. clubs. receiving rave revues by the media and local press. SirReal can be heard on their latest CD release project called <u>"Johari's Window"</u>.

Foreword

Merry Christmas! and welcome to my edition of
"Rockin' Christmas for Five String Bass".
This book is arranged in a few different approaches for the
bass guitar:

> * <u>First</u> it has been arranged for a **bass duet**, one
>   player will perform the main bass lines, which
>   are written in the bass clef. The second player
>   will perform the main melody, which is
>   written in the treble clef. This arrangement is
>   designed for those whom wish to develop their
>   treble clef sight reading as well as bass clef
>   reading.
> * The <u>second</u> is arranged for **two hand tapping**.
>   Most of the notes and tab is arranged to allow
>   left and right hand interdependence.
> * The <u>third</u> arrangement is for a **bass trio**. One
>   player plays the actual polyphonic chord much
>   as a guitarist. The second player will play the
>   written bass lines in bass clef. And the third
>   player will play the main melody written in
>   treble clef.

For the guitar players, my good friend and band mate Dave
Celentano has written **"Rockin' Christmas for Guitar"**. It
contains the same twelve songs and keys as this book. Dave
and I designed our books this way to give bass and guitar
players a set of Christmas songs they could learn and
perform together live.

Symbols and Terms

About The Chord Diagrams:

The chord diagrams are laid out much like a guitar chord diagram with the exception that these charts are to be played on the bass guitar. The illustrations in this book are mere examples of different chord voicing's that can be applied to the songs. You might want to experiment with some voicing's of your own. I've illustrated my examples for easy fingerings to very complex to give you added finger stretching and increased dexterity. (You should use the fingerings that are the easiest and most economical to make the proper chord changes per song).

Symbols to Know:

X= An X means the string or strings is not sounded.

A number, for example, 15, beside the chord diagram (the fret marker), shows you the correct fret to voice the chord

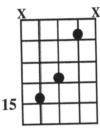

About the Chord Inversions:

A chord inversion is when the root of the chord is substituted by another note in the chord's bass or lowest pitched note position. Example:

> **CMaj. 7**
> Standard version= C-(lowest pitch in chord, or Root position), then, E-G-B, positioned in higher pitch ranges around the Root.
> **CMaj. 7**
> 1st Inversion= E-in Root position, then, C-G-B, arranged around the E.
> 2nd Inversion= G-in Root position, then, C-E-B, arranged around the G.
> 3rd Inversion= B-in Root position, then, C-E-G, arranged around the B.

You can arrange each chord's notes in any order you desire to give the song a different tone characteristic.

I have indicated the type of inversion used in my arrangements by placing 1st, 2nd, or 3rd over the chord diagram.

God Rest Ye Merry Gentlemen

Traditional

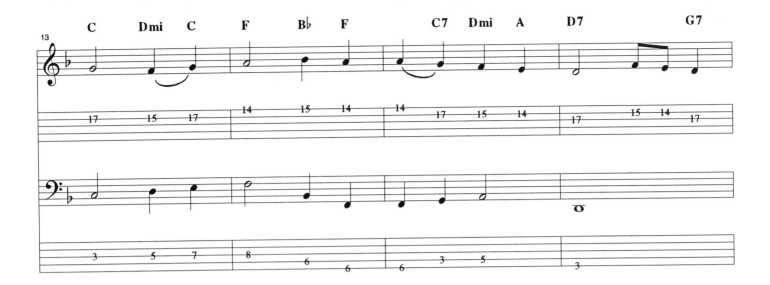

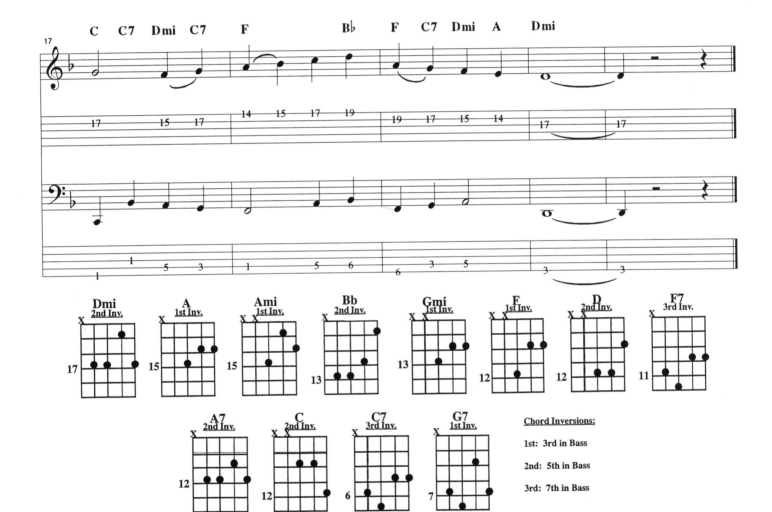

Chord Inversions:

1st: 3rd in Bass

2nd: 5th in Bass

3rd: 7th in Bass

GOD REST YOU MERRY, GENTLEMEN

God rest you merry, gentlemen,
Let nothing you dismay,
Remember Christ our Saviour
Was born on Christmas day;
To save us all from Satan's power
When we were gone astray.

Chorus:
O tidings of comfort and joy,
comfort and joy,
O tidings of comfort and joy.

In Bethlehem in Jewry
This blessed Babe was born,
And laid within a manger
Upon this blessed morn;
The which His mother Mary
Did nothing take in scorn:

Chorus

From God our heavenly Father
A blessed angel came,
And unto certain shepherds
Brought tidings of the same,
How that in Bethlehem was born
The Son of God by name:

Chorus

Hark! the Herald Angels Sing

Music by: Felix Mendelssohn

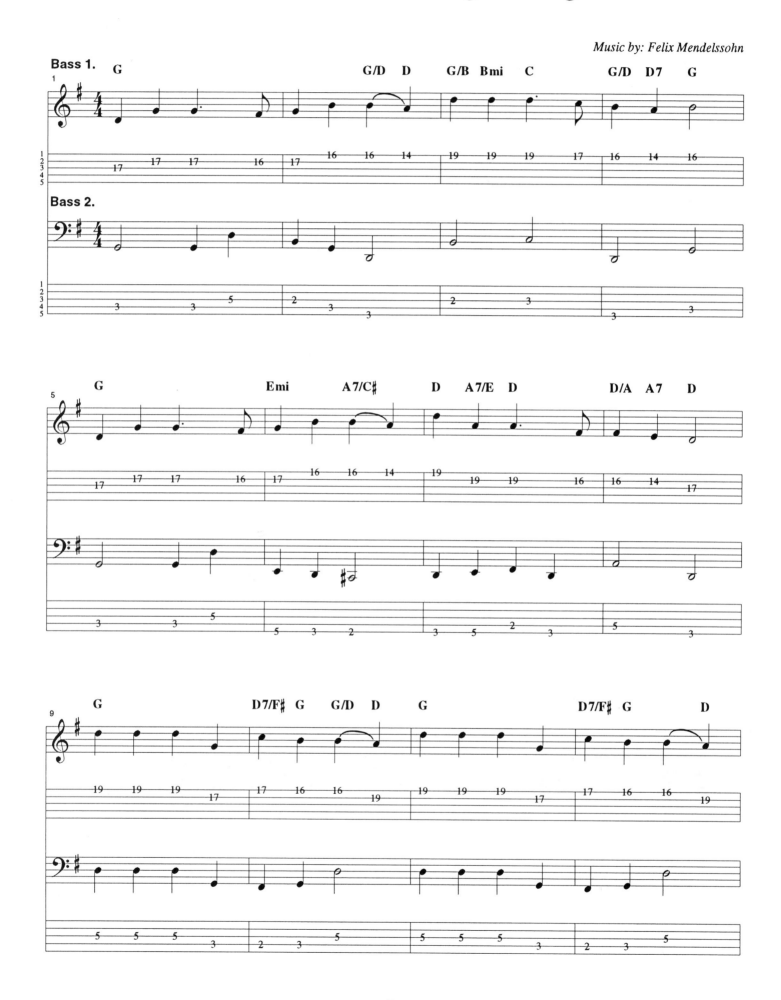

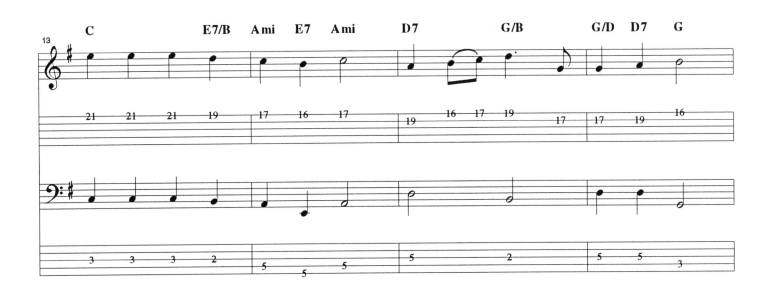

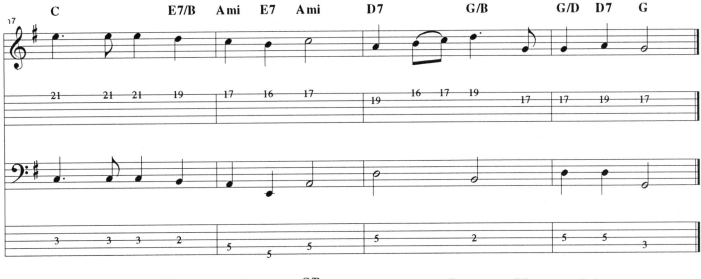

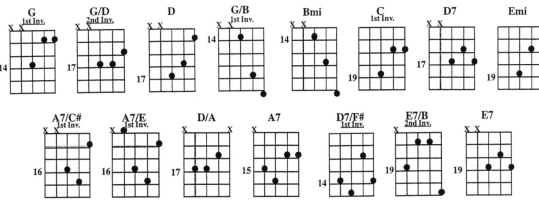

HARK! THE HERALD ANGELS SING

Hark! the herald angels sing
Glory to the new-born King,
Peace on earth, and mercy mild,
God and sinners reconciled.
Joyful, all ye nations, rise,
Join the triumph of the skies,
With th' angelic host proclaim,
Christ is born in Bethlehem;
Hark! the herald angels sing
Glory to the new-born King.

Hail the heaven-born Prince of Peace!
Hail the Sun of Righteousness!
Light and life to all He brings,
Risen with healing in His wings.
Mild He lays His glory by,
Born that man no more may die,
Born to raise the sons of earth,
Born to give them second birth.
Hark! the herald angels sing
Glory to the new-born King.

Christ, by highest heaven adored,
Christ, the everlasting Lord,
Late in time behold Him come,
Offspring of a Virgin's womb!
Veled in flesh the Godhead see;
Hail th'incarnate Deity!
Pleased as Man with men to dwell,
Jesus our Immanuel.
Hark! the herald angels sing
Glory to the new-born King.

What Child Is This?

(Greensleeves)

Traditional

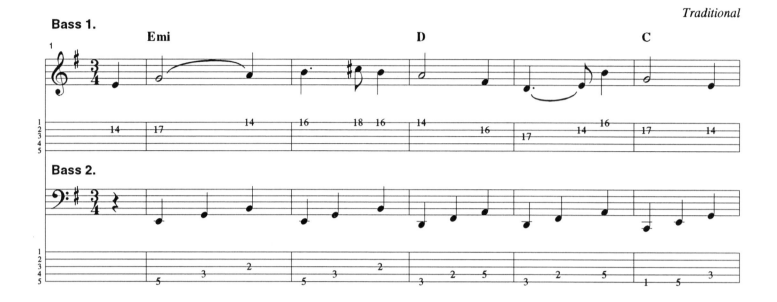

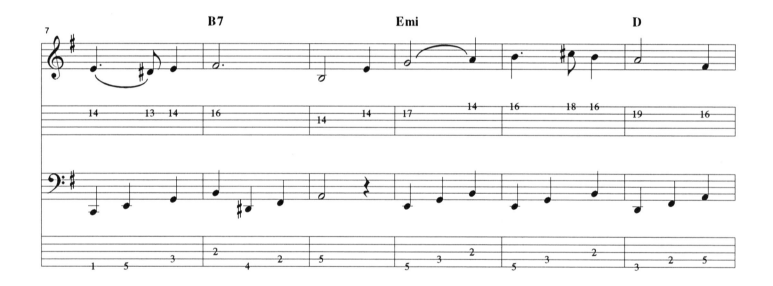

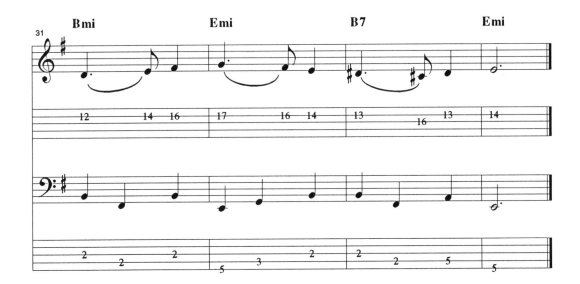

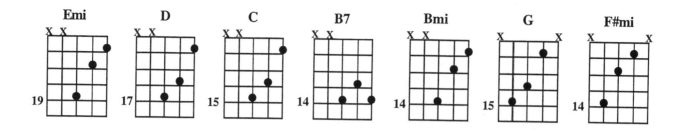

WHAT CHILD IS THIS?

What Child is this, who, laid to rest,
On Mary's lap is sleeping?
Whom angels greet with anthems sweet,
While shepherds watch are keeping?

Chorus:
This, this is Christ the King,
Whom shepherds guard and angels sing:
Haste, Haste to bring Him laud,
the Babe, The Son of Mary.

Why lies He is such mean estate
Where ox and ass are feeding?
Good Christian, fear: for sinners here
The silent Word is pleading.

Chorus

So bring Him incense, gold and myrrh,
Come, peasant, King, to own Him.
The King of kings salvation brings,
Let loving hearts enthrone Him.

Chorus

HOW LONG TO KEEP THE CHRISTMAS TREE: A VISUAL GUIDE

CHRISTMAS OLD TIME
YULE-TIDE FOLK CHARMS

According to ancient traditions in many lands, Christmas is the time when magical charms work best. Listed below are a few old customs that you might want to revive this year. They many not bring you health, happiness, and prosperity, a few are guaranteed to bring you notoriety in your neighborhood.

* Beat the fruit trees with a green switch on Christmas night, and they will bear more fruit the following year.

* On Christmas Eve thrash the garden with a flail (threshing tool), wearing only a shirt, and the crops will grow well.

* On Christmas day hang a wash cloth on a hedge, then groom the horses with it to make them grow fat.

* Burn elder wood on Christmas Eve and all the witches and sorcerers of the neighborhood will be revealed to you.

* Carry nothing forth from the house on Christmas day until something has been brought in order to avoid bad luck.

* Steal some hay the night before Christmas and give it to the cattle. They will thrive, and you will not be caught in any thefts for a whole year.

* All who help to bring in the Yule log will be protected from witchcraft the following year.

* Save a piece of the Yule log and keep it under the bed to protect the house from fire and lightning.

* Hang mistletoe over the door of the byre (cow barn) to protect the cattle from disease.

* Wear something sewed with the thread spun on Christmas Eve and no vermin (lice etc.) will stick to you.

The First Noel

Traditional

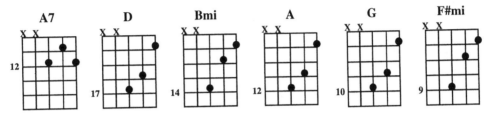

THE FIRST NOEL

The first noel the angel did say
Was to certain poor shepherds in fields as they lay;
In fields where they lay, keeping their sheep,
On a cold winter's night that was so deep:

Chorus:
Noel, Noel, Noel, Noel,
Born is the King of Israel!

They looked up and saw a star
Shining in the east, beyond them far,
And to the earth it gave great light,
And so it continued both day and night:

Chorus

And by the light of that same star,
Three wise men came from country far;
To seek for a King was their intent,
And to follow the star wherever it went:

Chorus

This star drew nigh to the north-west,
O'er Bethlehem it took its rest,
And there it did both stop and stay
Right over the place where Jesus lay:

Chorus

Then entered in those wise men three
Full reverently upon their knee,
And offered there in His presence
Their gold and myrrh and frankincense:

Chorus

Then let us all with one accord
Sing praises to our heavenly Lord
That hath made heaven and earth of nought,
And with his blood mankind hath bought:

Chorus

O Christmas Tree

Traditional

O CHRISTMAS TREE

O Christmas tree, O Christmas tree!
O evergreen unchanging!
Your branches green in summertime,
Still cheer us in our wintertime.
O Christmas tree, O Christmas tree!
O evergreen unchanging!

O Christmas tree, O Christmas tree!
You fill our hearts with gladness.
At Christmas time your lovely sight
Fills all our spirits with delight.
O Christmas tree, O Christmas tree!
You fill our hearts with gladness.

Joy to the World

Music by: Lowell Mason

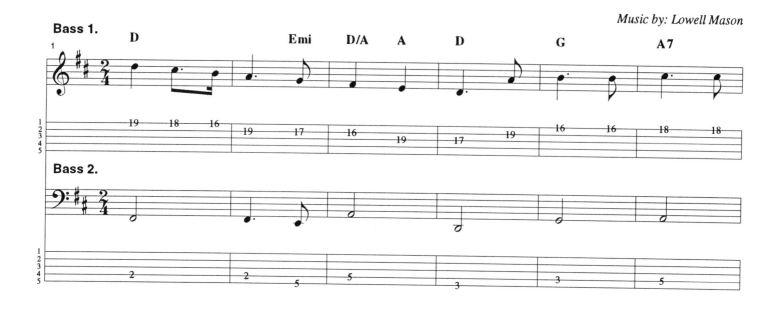

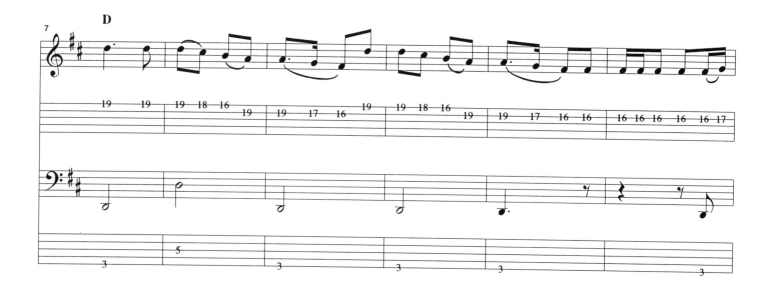

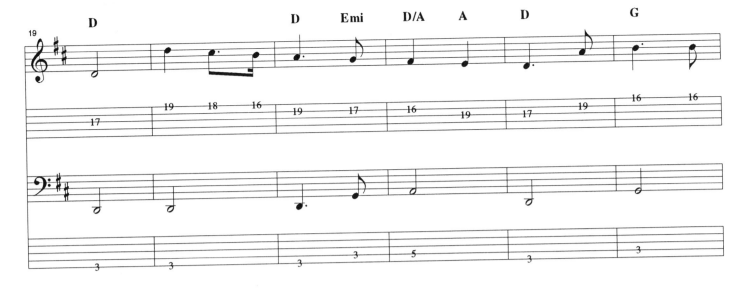

JOY TO THE WORLD

Joy to the world! The Lord is come;
Let earth receive her King;
Let ev'ry heart prepare Him room
And heav'n and nature sing,
And heav'n and nature sing
And heav'n, and heav'n and nature sing.

Joy to the world! The Saviour reigns;
Let men their songs employ;
While fields and floods, rocks, hills and plains
Repeat the sounding joy.

He rules the world with truth and grace,
And makes the nations prove
The glories of His righteousness,
And wonders of His love.

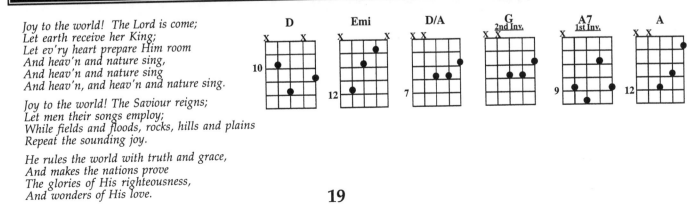

Deck the Hall

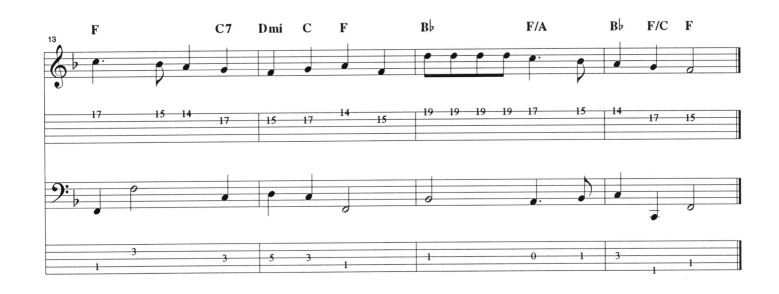

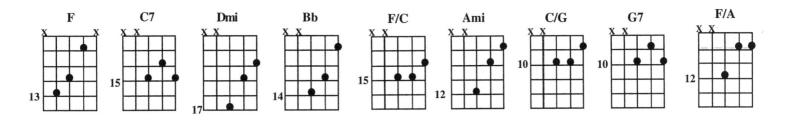

DECK THE HALLS

Deck the hall with boughs of holly,
Fa la la la la, la la la la.
"Tis the season to be jolly,
Fa la la la la, la la la la.
Don we now our gay apparel,
Fa la la la, la la la,
Troll the ancient Yuletide Carol,
Fa la la la la, la la la la.

See the blazing Yule before us,
* Fa la etc.*
Strike the harp and join the chorus,
Follow me in merry measure,
While I tell of Yuletide treasure.

Fast away the old year passes,
* Fa la etc.*
Hail the new, ye lads and lasses,
Sing we joyous all together,
Heedless of the wind and weather.

Carol of the Bells

Traditional

Bass 1.

Bass 2.

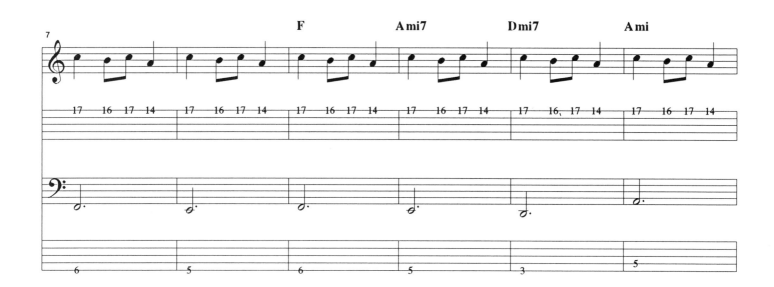

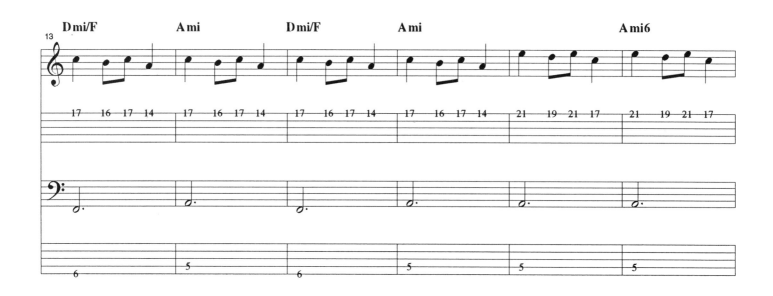

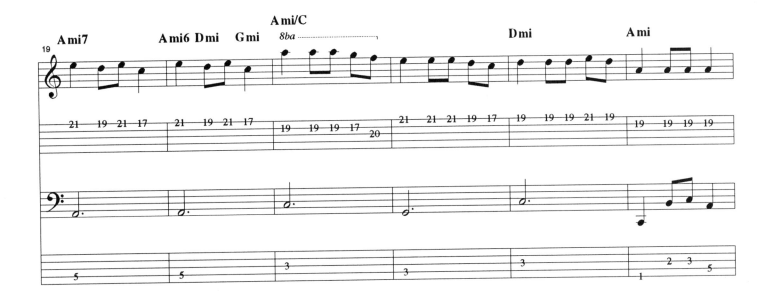

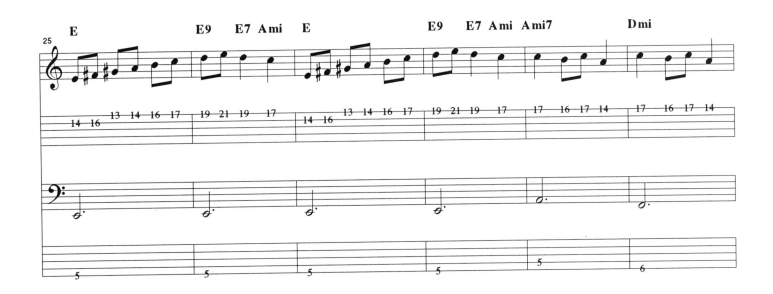

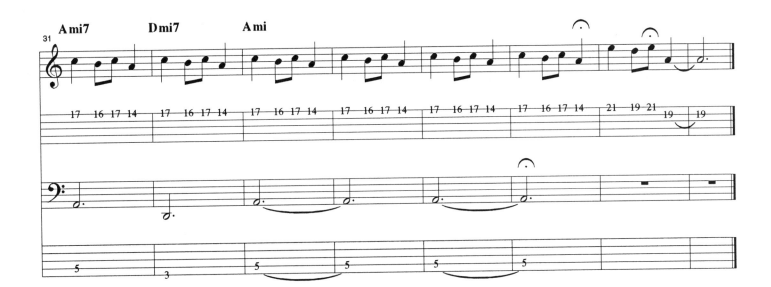

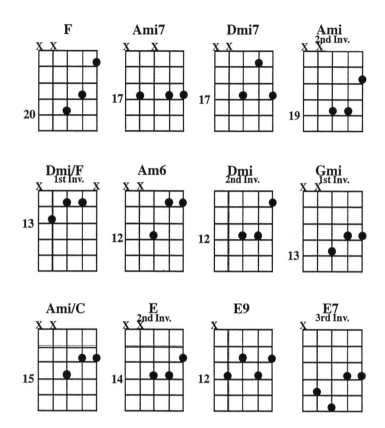

CAROL OF THE BELLS

Hark! How the bells; sweet silver bells, all seem to say,
"Throw cares away."
Christmas is here, bringing good cheer to young and old,
meek and the bold.
Ding, dong, ding, dong,
that is their song,
with joyful ring, all caroling.
One seems to hear words of good cheer from ev'rywhere
filling the air.
O, how they pound, raising the sound,
o'er hill and dale, telling their tale.
Gaily they ring, while people sing
song of good cheer, Christmas is here!

Merry, merry, merry, merry Christmas!
Merry, merry, merry, merry, Christmas!
On, on they send, on, with-out end,
their joyful tone to ev'ry home.
Ding, dong, ding, dong.

Silent Night

Music by: Joseph Mohr
and Franz Gruber

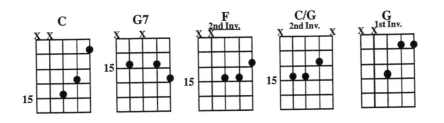

SILENT NIGHT

Silent night, holy night!
All is calm all is bright
Round yon Virgin mother and Child.
Holy Infant so tender and mild,
Sleep in heavenly peace,
Sleep in heavenly peace.

Silent night, holy night!
Shepherds first saw the light,
Heard resounding clear and long,
Far and near, the angel song:
Christ the Saviour is here.

Silent night, holy night !
Son of God, oh how bright
Love is smiling from Thy face!
Peals for us the hour of grace.
Christ our Saviour is born.

O Come All Ye Faithful

Music by: John Reading

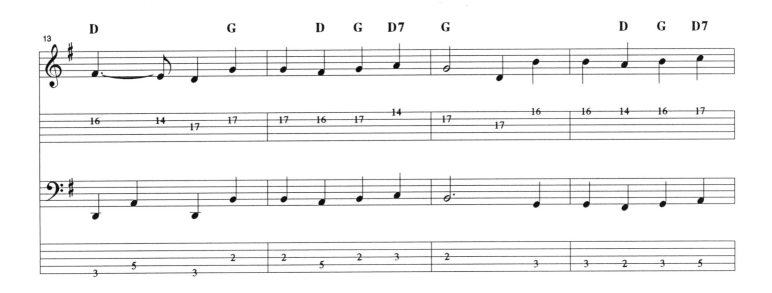

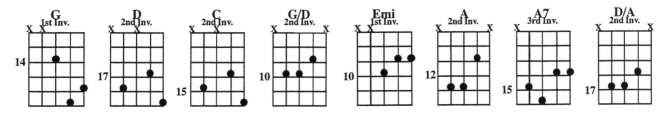

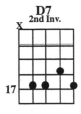

O COME, ALL YE FAITHFUL

O come, all ye faithful,
Joyful and triumphant,
O come ye, O come ye to Bethlehem;
Come and behold Him
Born the King of angels:

Chorus:
O come, let us adore Him,
O come, let us adore Him,
O come, let us adore Him,
Christ the Lord.

True God of True God,
Light of Light eternal,
Lo! He abhors not the Virgin's womb;
Son of the Father,
Begotten not created:

Chorus

Sing, choirs of angels,
Sing in exultation,
Sing all ye citizens of heaven above,
Sing ye, 'All glory
To god in the highest'.

Chorus

Yea, Lord, we greet Thee,
Born this happy morning;
Jesu, to Thee be glory given,
Word of the Father,
Now in flesh appearing:

Chorus

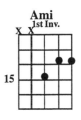

We Wish You A Merry Christmas

Traditional

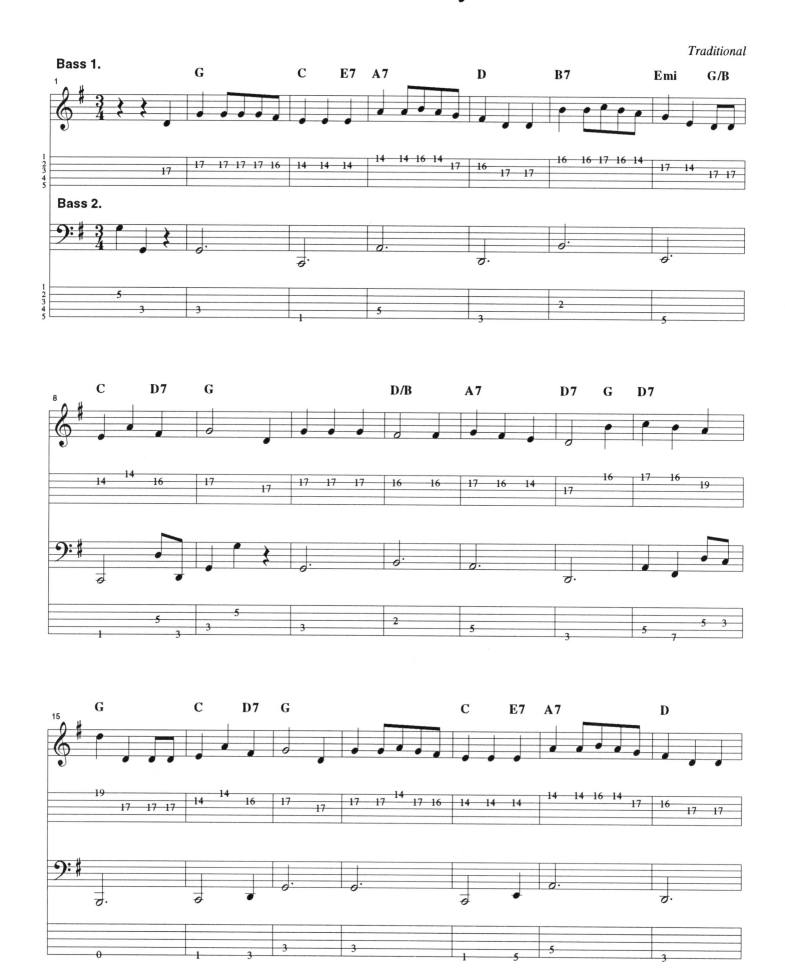

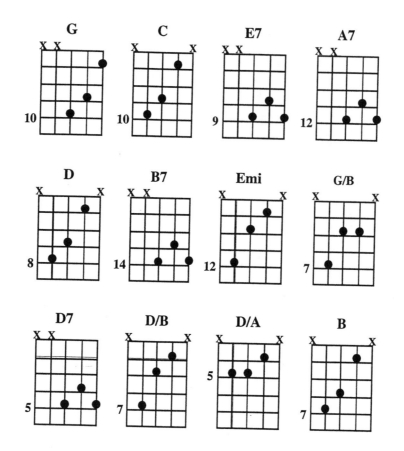

WE WISH YOU A MERRY CHRISTMAS

We wish you a merry Christmas,
We wish you a merry Christmas,
We wish you a merry Christmas
And a happy New Year.

Chorus:
Good tidings we bring
To you and your kin.
We wish you a merry Christmas
And a happy New Year.

Now bring us some figgy pudding. (3 times)
And bring some out here!

Chorus

For we all like figgy pudding, (3 times)
So bring some out here!

Chorus

And we won't go till we get some! (3 times)
So bring some out here!

Chorus

We wish you a merry Christmas, (3 times)
And a happy New Year.

The Twelve Days of Christmas

Traditional

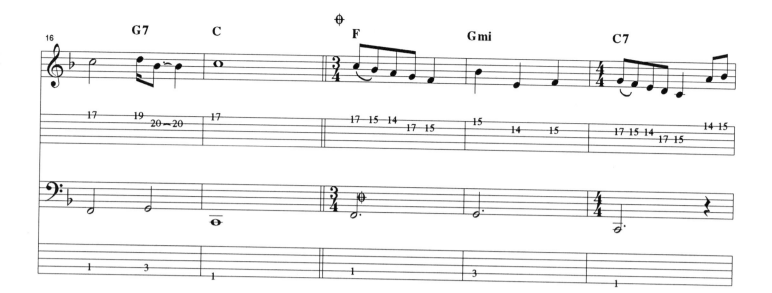

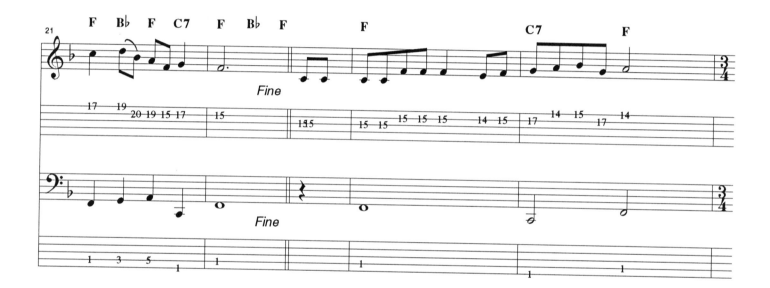

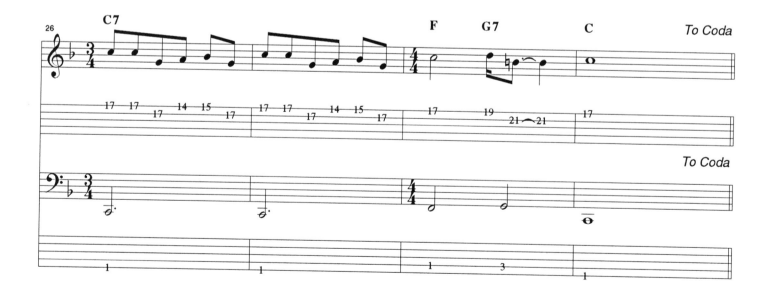

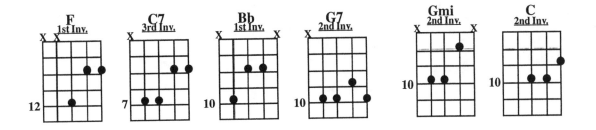

THE TWELVE DAYS OF CHRISTMAS

On the first day of Christmas my true love gave to me
A partridge in a pear tree.
On the second day of Christmas my true love gave to me
Two turtle doves, and a partridge in a pear tree.

"On the third day", " On the fourth day", etc.

3. *Three French hens*
4. *Four mockingbirds*
5. *Five golden rings*
6. *Six geese a-laying*
7. *Seven swans a-swimming*
8. *Eight maids a-milking*
9. *Nine ladies waiting*
10. *Ten lords a-leaping*
11. *"Leven pipers piping*
12. *Twelve drummers drumming*

35

Other 5 string Bass Books
by Brian Emmel

Centerstream Publishing P.O.Box 5450 Fullerton, CA 92635

5-String Bass Method*
by Brian Emmel
Centerstream Publications
The 5 string bass is rapidly growing into the future and this is your handbook to meet it there. Besides discussing how to adapt to the differences in the 5 string versus 4, this book explores the various ways of using the 5-string, practice tips, different techniques, and practical applications to various genres demonstrated through songs on the accompanying cassette.
_____00000134 Book/Cassette Pack $15.95

Scales and Modes for the 5-String Bass
by Brian Emmel
Centerstream Publications
foreword by Mark Egan
The most comprehensive and complete scale book written especially for the 5-string-bass. Divided into 4 main sections: 1) Scale Terminology 2) Scales 3) Fingerboard chart and diatonic triads 4) Scale to Chord Guide - tying it all together and showing what scale to use over various chords.
_____00000146..$9.95

CREATING RHYTHM STYLES FOR 5-STRING BASS WITH DRUM ACCOMPANIMENT
by Brian Emmel
Centerstream Publications
This book is designed for bassists to program the written drum grooves into a drum machine and develop a working knowledge over the rhythms and various styles. Drummers can play the written patterns along with a bassist and both can elaborate their playing skills over each example. The accompaniment CD allows you to fade out the bass guitar part on the left channel or the drums on the right channel.
00000162 Book/CD Pack $17.95

Other Books From CENTERSTREAM Publishing

CENTERSTREAM Publishing - P.O. Box 5450 - Fullerton CA 92635

Guitar Special Interest

Guitar Legends – The Evolution of the Guitar from Fender to G&L
by George Fullerton
Centerstream Publishing
The name Fender has become synonomous with guitar. The work of Leo Fender revolutionized the instrument and has influenced nearly every modern guitarist. This book by Leo's best friend and partner in G&L examines the life of the man behind these instruments. It features photos (including 16 pages of color!) never before published. You'll see the barn where Leo was born, the first Fender plant, the earliest instruments he created, and many other rare photos. ISBN #0-931759-69-2
00000156.......................................$24.95

Tommy Tedesco – Confessions Of A Guitar Player – An Autobiography
Centerstream Publishing
Tommy Tedesco is the most recorded guitarist in the history of the music business. His four-decade career has earned him a reputation among his peers as one of the world's best musicians. His contributions have been instrumental in shaping the sound of popular music. This book covers Tommy's life story and includes lots of studio photos and quotes from some of the world's most famous musicians. ISBN #0-931759-71-4
00000158.......................................$24.95

Gretsch – The Guitars of the Fred Gretsch Co.
by Jay Scott
Centerstream Publications
This is the comprehensive, must-own owner's or collector's manual for any Gretsch fan. It uncovers the history of the guitars through 32 pages of color photos, hundreds of black & white photos, and forewords by Fred Gretsch, George Harrison, Randy Bachman, Brian Setzer and Duane Eddy. It contains 30 chapters covering each Gretsch model in depth and a section of patent numbers and drawings for collectors. Find out what makes the essential "Rockabilly" guitar such a collector's item and such an icon of popular music history.
_____00000142 286 pages.........................$35.00

Songs Of The Cowboy
Compiled by Ron Middlebrook
Centerstream Publications
This unique book celebrates the romance attached to the cowboy and his free roaming life style. By combining classic cowboy songs, trivia, photos, articles and diagrams with current cowboy songwriters' songs, this book pays special tribute to our Western musical heritage.
_____00000129...$12.95

SAXOPHONE

Contemporary Saxophone
by John Laughter
Centerstream Publications
Contemporary Saxophone is a highly recommended book/cassette package for the intermediate sax player or any wind instrumentalist beginning to learn improvisation. The improvisation studies are laid out in a very logical order, dealing with the simple concepts of harmony. Excellent for the beginning soloist!
_____00000144...$15.95

GUITAR

OVER THE TOP
by Dave Celentano
Centerstream Publications
A new book/CD pack by Dave Celentano for guitarists who want to concentrate on their two-hand tapping technique.

00000166 Book/CD Pack $17.95

ELECTRIC BLUES GUITAR
by Derek Cornett
Centerstream Publications
An introduction to the most commonly used scales and techniques for the modern blues player, complete with CD. Includes musical examples to show how scales are used in improvisation, and play-along tunes that provide a "hands-on" start to improvisation.
00000165 Book/CD Pack $17.95

Survival Licks & Bar Room Tricks*
by Mark & J.R.
Centerstream Publications
A survival guide for today's music scene – from learning how to solo in a variety of styles to how to protect yourself from flying bottles. After reading this book, you will be equipped with the knowledge and confidence it takes to pull any gig off. Includes country, blues, rock, metal and jazz fusion licks in notes and tab.
_____00000133...$8.95

Rock Licks*
by Dave Celentano
Centerstream Publications
40 licks to help the guitarist stand out in the band. Discover all the styles with this book – blues, two-hand tapping, basic rock, speed and arpeggio licks – plus, Dave plays all of the examples on the accompanying cassette at slow and fast speeds.
_____00000112 Book/Cassette Pack $15.95

5-STRING BASS

5-String Bass Method*
by Brian Emmel
Centerstream Publications
The 5 string bass is rapidly growing into the future and this is your handbook to meet it there. Besides discussing how to adapt to the differences in the 5 string versus 4, this book explores the various ways of using the 5-string, practice tips, different techniques, and practical applications to various genres demonstrated through songs on the accompanying cassette.
_____00000134 Book/Cassette Pack $15.95

Scales and Modes for the 5-String Bass
by Brian Emmel
Centerstream Publications
foreword by Mark Egan
The most comprehensive and complete scale book written especially for the 5-string-bass. Divided into 4 main sections: 1) Scale Terminology 2) Scales 3) Fingerboard chart and diatonic triads 4) Scale to Chord Guide - tying it all together and showing what scale to use over various chords.
_____00000146...$9.95

HARMONICA

METHODS

Blues & Rock Harmonica
by Glenn Weiser
Centerstream Publications
Book/cassette package for beginners to learn blues & rock improvisation. Includes explanations of scales, modes, chords & other essential elements of music. The cassette features riffs & solos plus demonstrations and a blues jam to play along with.
_____00000127...$16.95

Drum

Drum Programming
by Ray F. Badness
Foreword by Mark Simon
Centerstream Publications
This is your complete guide to programming and thinking like a *drummer* – not a drum machine. Instead of providing merely instructions for you to program into your machine, this book is a direct and mathematical approach to learning how to drum and how to best emulate a drum kit on a prerecorded track. By following this book you will get an understanding of the drum kit that takes many drummers years to learn – and that will lead to more realistic programming and better results!
00000138...$9.95